Betsy Ross

American Patriot

Colonial Leaders

Lord Baltimore *English Politician and Colonist*

Benjamin Banneker *American Mathematician and Astronomer*

William Bradford *Governor of Plymouth Colony*

Benjamin Franklin *American Statesman, Scientist, and Writer*

Anne Hutchinson *Religious Leader*

Cotton Mather *Author, Clergyman, and Scholar*

William Penn *Founder of Democracy*

John Smith *English Explorer and Colonist*

Miles Standish *Plymouth Colony Leader*

Peter Stuyvesant *Dutch Military Leader*

Revolutionary War Leaders

Benedict Arnold *Traitor to the Cause*

Nathan Hale *Revolutionary Hero*

Alexander Hamilton *First U.S. Secretary of the Treasury*

Patrick Henry *American Statesman and Speaker*

Thomas Jefferson *Author of the Declaration of Independence*

John Paul Jones *Father of the U.S. Navy*

Thomas Paine *Political Writer*

Paul Revere *American Patriot*

Betsy Ross *American Patriot*

George Washington *First U.S. President*

Betsy Ross

American Patriot

Susan Martins Miller

Arthur M. Schlesinger, jr.
Senior Consulting Editor

Chelsea House Publishers

Philadelphia

Produced by 21st Century Publishing and Communications, Inc.
New York, NY. http://www.21cpc.com

CHELSEA HOUSE PUBLISHERS
Editor in Chief Stephen Reginald
Production Manager Pamela Loos
Director of Photography Judy L. Hasday
Art Director Sara Davis
Managing Editor James D. Gallagher

Staff for *BETSY ROSS*
Project Editor/Publishing Coordinator Jim McAvoy
Associate Art Director Takeshi Takahashi
Series Design Keith Trego

The Chelsea House World Wide Web address is
http://www.chelseahouse.com

First Printing
1 3 5 7 9 8 6 4 2

Library of Congress Cataloging-in-Publication Data

Miller, Susan Martins.
Betsy Ross / by Susan Martins Miller.
80 pp. cm. — (Revolutionary War Leaders series)
Includes bibliographical references and index.
Summary: A biography of the Philadelphia seamstress who helped
design and make the first flag to represent the United States of America.
ISBN 0-7910-5360-1 (hc)   ISBN 0-7910-5703-8 (pb)
1. Ross, Betsy, 1752–1836—Juvenile literature. 2. Revolutionaries—United
States—Biography—Juvenile literature. 3. United States—History—
Revolution, 1775–1783—Flags—Juvenile literature. 4. Flags—United
States—History—18th century—Juvenile literature. [1. Ross, Betsey,
1752-1836. 2. United States—History—Revolution, 1775–1783—Biography.
3. Flags—United States. 4. Women—Biography] I. Title. II. Series.
E302.6.R77M55   1999
973.3'1'092—dc21   99-25131
[B]   CIP

Publisher's Note: In Colonial and Revolutionary War America, there were no standard rules for spelling, punctuation, capitalization, or grammar. Some of the quotations that appear in the Colonial Leaders and Revolutionary War Leaders series come from original documents and letters written during this time in history. Original quotations reflect writing inconsistencies of the period.

Contents

The Pennsylvania State House was well known to Betsy Ross as she grew up in Philadelphia. Her father had helped build the tall bell tower. The ringing of the bell called people into the streets to hear important news.

Growing Up Quaker

Every morning, Elizabeth Griscom snatched her clothes off a peg and hurriedly got dressed. Every morning she wore a plain gray dress, a white apron, and a white cap. It did not take her long to decide what to wear. She had only a few clothes, and they were all the same. Many of her clothes were handed down from her six older sisters. Even when she got new clothes, they were the same. Her dress was always gray, and her apron and cap were always white.

Elizabeth moved quickly in the morning. Not a moment could be wasted. Her house was a busy place because she was part of a big family. There was always a lot of work to do. Even as a child, Elizabeth had chores to do each day. Wood had to be chopped to warm the family's home and cook meals. The kitchen was busy and crowded. The family made their own candles and soap. Everyone in the family did his or her part.

Elizabeth, who was also called Betsy, had 16 brothers and sisters! At the time that Betsy lived, many families were large. Often some of the children died when they were babies. Several of Betsy's brothers and sisters died when they were little.

Betsy was the eighth child in the Griscom family. She was born on January 1, 1752, in West Jersey, Pennsylvania. As she grew up her chores often included taking care of her many younger brothers and sisters. It seemed that her mother was always taking care of a new baby or expecting another one. But the small Griscom house was filled with love, and there was always room for a new member of the family.

Long before Betsy was born, her great-grandfather Andrew Griscom had moved from faraway England to Philadelphia, Pennsylvania. He was a carpenter, and he was very successful. He was also a **Quaker**. The Quakers had very strong beliefs about God, but their beliefs were different from those of many of the other people in England. Instead of churches, they had meeting houses. Their gathering was called a meeting.

Quakers did not have ministers to lead a church service or preach a sermon. Instead they waited for God's Spirit to speak to people in the congregation. This was called the Inner Light. The Quakers also did not play music. They waited in silence for the Inner Light.

They wanted to live a simple, peaceful life. They wanted to worship God in their own way. The Quakers were also called Friends, or the **Society of Friends**.

Because of their unusual beliefs, the Quakers did not fit in well with the people who belonged to the other churches in England. Many Quakers decided to move to America. They settled in the Pennsylvania **colony**. A man named William Penn worked hard to make a place where the Quakers and their beliefs would be welcome. He called this the Holy Experiment. Andrew Griscom came from England to America to live with other Quakers and be part of the Holy Experiment.

The king of England ruled Great Britain as well as the American colonies, including Pennsylvania. But he lived across the ocean. It took weeks for any news to cross the ocean on a ship. People like Andrew Griscom hoped the king would not bother them very much. Andrew purchased almost 500 acres of land north of Philadelphia and began his new life.

Andrew Griscom married and had a family. He taught his son how to be a carpenter. Andrew patiently showed his son how to use the tools and to be careful with every detail of the work. His son learned to be an excellent carpenter. Both Andrew and his son became

So that all people in the Pennsylvania colony could live together in peace, Quaker leader William Penn met with Native Americans and signed a treaty of friendship.

well known in Philadelphia for their skills.

Later, Andrew's grandson, Samuel, also became a carpenter. When Samuel grew older, he helped to build the bell tower at the Pennsylvania State House in Philadelphia. At the State House, a bronze bell rang to call the people into the streets to hear important announcements.

Samuel Griscom married Rebecca James, also a Quaker. Rebecca's father was a successful merchant. Samuel and Rebecca Griscom were Betsy's parents. By the time Betsy was born, her family had been in America for four generations, and they continued to live in the Quaker ways. When Betsy was two years old, the family moved from West Jersey back to Philadelphia, where her great-grandfather had first settled.

The Griscom family attended meetings with other Friends every Sunday and Thursday. (Sunday was called First Day, and Thursday was Fifth Day.) Everyone sat quietly for hours at a time. Even the youngest children had to learn to be very still during meetings. Betsy had never attended any other kind of house of worship. The Quaker ways were the only ways she knew.

Quaker children were not allowed to dance or to play music. They could not read story books. They were not allowed to play cards. Betsy's gray and white clothes were Quaker clothes, just like the ones that her mother and sisters wore. She would never be seen without her Quaker bonnet. In many ways, the Quakers lived separately from the city around them. Some people who were not Quakers thought the Quakers were too strict and serious. But with 17 children in the family, there was always plenty to do and someone to play with at the Griscom house. So Betsy did not mind that she was not allowed to dance or play music. She and her brothers and sisters could have picnics and hayrides in the summer. And in the winter they could go sledding and skating. Their imaginations were always at work.

When Betsy was a little girl, not all children went to school. Girls especially stayed home and learned to do housework. But Betsy did go to school. She went to the Friends' public school with many other Quaker children. The school days were long, and she worked hard. Betsy studied for eight hours a day. She even went to school on Saturday.

Betsy loved reading and writing. Even more,

Like other children in colonial America, young Betsy spent long hours in school. She learned to read and write as well as prepare for a trade.

she loved to sew. She stitched samplers, quilts, and clothes. All of the children in the Friends' school learned a trade. Betsy's trade was sewing. Although she went to school for eight hours each day, she got to spend much of that time working on her stitches. When she was very young, other people saw that she had a talent for sewing. And

Betsy knew that she wanted to sew when she grew up. She looked forward to the day when she could work in an **upholstery** shop.

When Betsy was 12 years old, her schooling came to an end. Most girls stopped going to school at this age. Then it was time for them to learn to run a household. They would have to be ready when the time came to be wives and mothers. Betsy spent most of her time helping with chores for the large family. She learned to cook, clean, and spin thread. She dipped candle wicks in hot wax and boiled fat and wood ashes to make lye for soap. Betsy learned to wash, iron, and mend clothing. She shopped for the things that the family needed, baked bread with her mother, and learned to handle money. Her childhood was over. It was time to grow up.

In that same year, 1764, the Griscom family moved into a large brick house on Arch Street in Philadelphia. Betsy's father had built the house. Now there was room for the growing family.

By the time Betsy was a teenager, colonists were talking of independence. In response, the king showed his authority by sending thousands of soldiers on ships like these, which are entering Boston Harbor.

From Apprentice to Shopkeeper

When Betsy was old enough, her father arranged for her to learn a trade in a shop. She would be able to earn money to take care of herself. Even if she got married, she would need to be able to earn money.

Philadelphia was not a quiet city anymore. It was not a place where the Quakers could live their simple life and not worry about what went on around them. None of the American colonies were quiet.

During Betsy's teenage years, Philadelphia and many other American cities became restless. Many of the leaders believed it was time for the colonies to become a nation of their own. They would be separate from Great Britain. Then the king would not be able to make laws for America. Instead, the people in America would make their own laws. When they paid taxes, the money would go to their own country, and not to the king. As the restlessness grew, more and more people began to think there was going to be a war between the colonies and Great Britain.

Many British soldiers were stationed all over the colonies, especially in cities that had seaports. The king wanted to remind the people in America that they were still colonists. There were 13 colonies in America. They were New Hampshire, Massachusetts, Connecticut, Rhode Island, New York, New Jersey, Pennsylvania (where Betsy lived), Maryland, Delaware, Virginia, North Carolina, South Carolina, and Georgia.

The Quakers were **pacifists**. They did not believe in war. They would not carry **muskets** or shoot at British soldiers. Many of the Quaker merchants carried on with their business. They did not want to cause trouble with the British or other Americans. But the tension between the colonies and Britain grew. Many things that people used daily came from Britain and were taxed by the king. If colonists fought the British, then they would not be able to get the things that they needed. As the king increased taxes, the prices on food and household items in the colonies continued to go up. Soon they became very expensive. As Betsy became an adult, she would need to be able to earn an income to pay for these things.

Betsy's father arranged for her to be an **apprentice** in an upholstery shop owned by John Webster. Webster's shop was famous in Philadelphia. This was a very good chance for Betsy to improve her sewing skills. In colonial times upholsterers covered furniture with fabric, but they also did many other kinds of sewing. Betsy would soon be working on tablecloths, clothing, quilts, flags, umbrellas, and many other things. John Webster was also a Quaker, and he welcomed Betsy Griscom into his shop.

An apprentice works with, and learns from, people who are experts at a job. Usually an apprenticeship lasted for several years. At the time that Betsy lived, apprentices were not paid for their work but were given food and shelter. Being an apprentice was like going to school. The apprentice was supposed to concentrate on learning as much as possible.

In the upholstery shop, Betsy's days were very long. She spent even more hours at work than she used to spend at school. When she first started working for Mr. Webster, she was given the easy jobs to do. Sometimes she did not even get to sew. Instead she helped keep the shop clean and ran errands. The longer she stayed, the more sewing work she was allowed to do. She enjoyed sewing with beautiful fabrics very much. Betsy quickly became skilled as an upholsterer.

One of the best parts of being an apprentice in John Webster's shop was making new friends. Betsy made a special friend. His name was John

Ross. John was another apprentice. It did not take them very long to find out that they liked many of the same things. They especially liked each other. They dreamed of the day when they finished their apprenticeships and would be able to open their own upholstery shop. John and Betsy fell in love with each other. They decided they would get married and open a shop together.

They had a big problem, however. John Ross was not a Quaker. The Quakers believed that they should marry only other Quakers. John's father was a minister in an **Anglican** church, which was the major church in Britain. The Quakers and the Anglicans had bad feelings about each other. But Betsy loved John. She had to choose between John Ross and the Society of Friends.

Betsy chose John. Betsy's parents did not approve of her decision to marry John. They tried to persuade Betsy that she was making the wrong decision. But Betsy would not change her mind. She knew she loved John and she wanted to marry him.

When John finished his apprenticeship at Mr. Webster's shop, he opened his own upholstery shop. This was what he had always dreamed of doing. Betsy was so proud of John. As soon as she could, she left Webster's shop and went to work for John. She hoped that they would be able to get married very soon.

A few months later, the time came for John and Betsy to get married. Betsy's parents still did not approve of John. Betsy knew that they would not help her with a wedding. If she was going to marry John, she would have to do it on her own. She was 21 years old now. She could make her own choices.

Betsy and John decided to **elope**. Betsy made all the arrangements. They would not get married in Philadelphia. Instead, they would cross the Delaware River to New Jersey and get married there. Betsy's sister Sarah was willing to help. Sarah's husband was a seaman who

Once married, Betsy and John Ross worked many hours to increase business at their upholstery shop on Chestnut Street.

could row John and Betsy across the river. They decided that November 4, 1773, would be their big day. They worked all day in the upholstery shop and put the plan into action after work. The couple secretly crossed the river in the dark of night. As soon as they arrived at the other side of the river, Betsy and John found the local justice of the peace. A few minutes later, they were husband and wife.

The newlyweds returned home quickly to their new business. Betsy helped out in the front of the shop. Unfortunately they did not have as much work as they wanted. It was hard to start a new upholstery business because Philadelphia already had many upholstery shops. John and Betsy were going to have to work hard to find some loyal customers.

After she got married, Betsy's relationship with her family was never the same. Her parents never accepted John and never approved of their marriage. Many of the Quakers wanted Betsy to admit that she had made a mistake. Betsy refused. She loved John. She did not think that marrying him was a mistake. The Society of Friends would not allow Betsy to be part of their meetings any longer. Betsy was "read out" of the Quaker group.

Even though she was no longer a Quaker, Betsy still wanted to worship God. Now she went to the Anglican church with John. She had to get used to the organ music and the minister's sermons. But there were new people to meet and new friends to share her life with. John and Betsy's pew at Christ Church was near the pew where George Washington often sat.

George Washington was one of the colonial leaders who thought that it was time for America to be its own nation. Washington often came to Philadelphia for meetings from his plantation home in Virginia.

All around John and Betsy, people were talking about a **revolt**. The colonists refused to pay unfair taxes to the king any longer. The king had just put a new tax on all tea from Britain. At the same time, he said the colonists must buy British tea and could not buy tea from anyone else.

The citizens of Boston, Massachusetts, were very angry. Ships carrying tea from Britain had arrived in the harbor. Some colonists dressed up to look like Native Americans and snuck aboard the ships. Once on the ships, being very careful not to damage anything else, they threw all the tea into the water. Many people gathered nearby to watch and cheer. The bold Bostonians' actions were called the Boston Tea Party, and news of the event soon spread to all the colonies.

The governor in Boston also watched the entire episode from his second-story window. He decided not to order the soldiers to stop the law breakers at this time. He was concerned because there were too many other ordinary citizens standing around who might accidentally get hurt. However, he did write a full report and sent it to the king.

When the king heard the news he got very angry. He decided that he was going to teach the colonists a lesson. He sent big warships with more soldiers to close Boston Harbor. No ship

As spectators cheer, Boston colonists angry over the tea tax board a British ship carrying tea. Disguised as Native Americans, the colonists threw hundreds of barrels of tea into Boston Harbor.

could use the harbor to load or unload any goods. Now the people who lived in Boston could not get the things they needed to live.

Many people in all 13 of the American colonies were absolutely furious with the king. They were about ready to revolt.

While Betsy and John worked hard at their new shop on Arch Street, people in Philadelphia were divided about independence from Britain. Many wanted to fight the British. Others, including most Quakers who did not believe in war, decided to remain loyal to Britain.

3

Loyalty in Philadelphia

About two years into their marriage, John and Betsy moved. They decided they needed to relocate their shop to a different part of Philadelphia. They moved from Chestnut Street to Arch Street, near the place where Betsy had grown up. But her family would still not accept her marriage to John.

Running a business became harder every day. John and Betsy had to buy a lot of fabric and supplies, and they did not have much money. They worked hard from early in the morning until late at night. Having their own shop was a dream that they shared. They wanted to do everything they could to make the dream come true.

Philadelphia was a very important American city at that time. When John and Betsy started their own business there, they had no idea what was going to happen. Philadelphia and many other cities and towns had always had British soldiers stationed there. They were sent there to make sure that the colonies followed the laws of Britain. But American colonists had different feelings and opinions about the British. John and Betsy would have to decide for themselves how they felt toward Britain.

Many people in the colonies were loyal to King George III. They thought of themselves as citizens of Britain, even though most of them had never been there. These people were called **Loyalists**.

Not everyone felt that way. More and more American colonists were becoming unhappy with King George. Many people thought that

Britain was not being fair to the colonies. America was no longer like a little child that needed to be told what to do all the time. The colonies had grown up, and they were ready to be on their own. The people who thought this way were called **Patriots**. They were patriotic and loyal to America.

The colonists began to organize. A group of Patriot leaders from different colonies held meetings in Philadelphia. At the meetings they discussed what to do about the problems with Britain. Should they insist that the king listen to them? If they all worked together, could they make him listen? Each meeting was called a Continental Congress.

At the Continental Congress, leaders from many of the colonies made a bold plan. They would tell the king that the colonies must be treated fairly. If he did not agree, then they would refuse to support him. They would no longer pay taxes and send money to Britain. And the colonists' ships would carry goods to and from anywhere in the world.

On September 6, 1774, the first Continental Congress met in Philadelphia, Pennsylvania. Forty-five delegates came to the meeting, representing 12 colonies. Only the colony of Georgia did not send a representative. The Congress was divided on one issue: one group wanted to fight and separate from Britain; the other wanted to stay in the British empire and find a peaceful settlement.

George Washington attended the meeting dressed in his army uniform. He spoke only once, but he was a very powerful presence. Soon after the Congress met, battles between colonists and British troops broke out. The war had begun.

These important meetings took place not very far from where Betsy and John lived and worked in Philadelphia.

No one really wanted a war. At first, the Patriots hoped that King George would read their letters and decide to be more fair. Unfortunately, that did not happen. Instead, the king made one new law after another—laws that continued to hurt the colonies. People like John and Betsy who were only trying to run their small businesses could not get the supplies they needed. King George and the leaders of Britain thought

Colonial leaders listen to a speaker at a meeting of the Continental Congress in Philadelphia. The representatives had to decide whether to fight Britain or remain loyal.

the colonies were not sending enough money to Britain.

Britain had been fighting with France for many years over who owned the land in America. Britain had to borrow a lot of money to pay for that war. It was deep in debt and needed the money to pay its bills. So Britain passed laws to tax everything in the colonies, from paper to tea. The colonists grew more angry and resentful. A war with Britain seemed to be the only way to prove to King George that they were serious.

In June 1775 the people of Philadelphia could no longer stand by without doing something. Colonists in Massachusetts had already fought two battles with the British.

George Washington thought it was time to help Massachusetts. He gathered **troops** in Philadelphia and began the long march toward Boston. The Revolutionary War had begun.

Quakers, like Betsy's family, believed that liberty was a gift from God and everyone had a right to it. However, they did not believe in war. Some of the people in Philadelphia who were not Quakers wished the Quakers would make up their minds. Were they loyal to King George or were they loyal to the colonies? Some Quakers decided that they were loyal to the colonies and would go to war against the

When Betsy's husband, John, decided to join the Patriot cause, he was one of thousands of ordinary people like these colonists who fought British soldiers to defend their liberty.

British. They called themselves the Fighting Quakers or **Free Quakers**. They did their part to help in the war effort.

John Ross believed in doing his part to protect Philadelphia. He took his turn as a guard on the waterfront. Men guarded the **ammunition** stored in a warehouse there. The ammunition must be ready at all times in case the war came to Philadelphia. Sometimes John patrolled the waterfront all night long. He would be there by himself until the sun came up the next day and another guard came to relieve him.

One night, a spark near the ammunition warehouse caused an explosion. John did not get away in time. Betsy was at home asleep when the explosion happened. Suddenly she woke up as she heard banging on her front door. She raced to open the door. John was injured. A group of men had carried him home to her.

But John was unconscious. Betsy could see that he was hurt very badly. She asked the men to carry John upstairs to their bed, where he would be more comfortable and she could care for him. There she sat by her husband's bedside for the next few days. She watched as he became weaker and weaker. There was nothing Betsy could do. There was nothing the doctor could do. Finally, on January 21, 1776, John Ross died from his injuries. Betsy Ross became a **widow**.

Betsy had some big decisions to make. Her parents wanted her to come home. Since she was no longer married to someone who was not a Quaker, she could go back to the Society of Friends. She could go back to her family. But Betsy did not choose to do this. She decided to carry on with the upholstery business that she and John had started together. She would live in the house and run the shop.

Even more, Betsy decided to do her part for the war, just as John had done. Her family had been in America for four generations. America was her country, not Britain. However she could help, she would do it.

As Americans fought the British, they needed a flag to represent their cause. Patriot leaders decided to change this Grand Union flag, which looked too much like the British flag, into a new flag to symbolize American independence. They asked Betsy Ross to make the flag.

4

A Mysterious Visit

Boston was taken over by the British. All around the colonies, American soldiers gathered and drilled and practiced. They wanted to be ready for the battles ahead of them.

George Washington was doing the best he could to train the American soldiers. But the American army did not have much money. It needed more money to pay for uniforms, guns, ammunition, food, and transportation for the soldiers. Winter had come. It was hard to move soldiers around so that they could be in the right places to fight.

The army was not well organized. Each colony

had its own **militia**, but the militias did not cooperate well with one another. They had to work together to successfully fight the British.

George Washington became commander of the American troops, called the Continental Army. Just before John Ross died, George Washington was in Boston. He led the American troops in battle against the British.

On January 1, 1776, George Washington ordered the Grand Union flag to be raised in Boston. This was the flag that he had chosen to represent the Americans. He hoped it would make the British see that the Americans were not going to give up. They would keep fighting. They would keep flying their flag.

The Grand Union flag looked very much like the British flag. It had all the same colors, and it had similar symbols, so when the Grand Union flag was raised, Loyalists and British troops in Boston thought that George Washington had surrendered. This was just the opposite of what he had done.

If America was to be its own nation, it needed its own flag. But no one could agree on exactly what the new flag should look like. Many people made lots of very interesting flags, with different colors and symbols. George Washington wanted America to have a flag that everyone would see and be proud of.

The Grand Union flag had six white strips on a red field, creating 13 stripes representing the 13 colonies. In the upper left corner, there was the red cross of Saint George, the symbol of England, and the white cross of Saint Andrew, the symbol of Scotland. Using this flag, the Americans hoped to show that they were still looking for justice within the British empire.

By June of 1776 Betsy Ross had been a widow for several months. She had kept her shop open the whole time. She sewed whatever people needed her to make for them. She probably even sewed some shirt ruffles for George Washington. They knew each other because they both went to the same church, so when Washington needed someone to make a flag, he thought of Betsy Ross.

George took some of his friends with him to

visit Betsy. They were a secret committee of the Continental Congress. They wanted Betsy to use her sewing skills for her country by making a flag.

Robert Morris was a delegate to the Continental Congress from Pennsylvania and one of the signers of the Declaration of Independence. He was called the "financier of the Revolution." He was a good friend of George Washington.

Whenever George Washington came to Philadelphia for meetings, he was a house guest in the Morris home. After Washington was elected the first president of the United States, he offered Morris the position as the first secretary of the treasury. Morris did not accept the offer, and the position went to Alexander Hamilton.

One of the men who came with George Washington to visit Betsy was Robert Morris. He came to America from Britain as a boy. At first, he thought that the colonies should not separate from Britain. Later he changed his mind and became one of the leaders of the American Revolution. Robert Morris helped Washington most by giving large amounts of money to the army. He asked other people to give money, too. The money they raised was used to buy food, ammunition, and all the other things the soldiers needed.

The other man who came with Washington was George Ross, John Ross's uncle. Like Robert Morris, George Ross was involved in Pennsylvania politics. He was also a lawyer. Betsy probably already knew George Ross because he was related to her husband. George Ross might have been the one to suggest that Betsy could sew the new flag that the committee wanted.

When the committee visited Betsy, they brought a sketch that showed their idea for the flag. It was square, with 13 stripes and 13 stars. Betsy liked the sketch, but she had some ideas for how it could be

George Ross was the son of a minister. He had a good education and became a lawyer. In 1774, he served in the first Continental Congress. At first, he supported the Loyalists. Later he changed his opinions and sided with the Patriots. George Ross was very popular with Pennsylvanians. Only Benjamin Franklin received more votes to be elected from Pennsylvania to the Congress. Ross was one of the signers of the Declaration of Independence. However, during the time he was in the Congress, he accomplished very little because of illness. Too sick to go on, he left the Congress in 1777 and died two years later.

Ships in the Continental Navy flew this flag of a rattlesnake ready to strike. The message warns the enemy not to come too close.

better. While many flags that flew on ships were square, Betsy thought this one should be a rectangle. And the stars Washington had drawn had six points. Betsy knew that stars with five points were much easier to cut and sew. She showed the committee how she could fold a piece of fabric in a special way. Then with just one snip, she could make a five-pointed star.

The committee agreed to the suggestions that Betsy made. They asked her to make a flag as quickly as she could. They did not want to wait any longer than necessary for the flag that would fly over the American soldiers. The committee made sure Betsy had the money she needed to buy supplies for making the flag.

Betsy began right away and worked as fast as she could. But sewing a large flag by hand, with strong, straight stitches, would take a long time. The very heavy wool fabric meant using special needles. She put aside the other work in her shop and concentrated on making the flag.

Betsy sewed 13 stripes. Seven were red, and six were white. Then, in one corner, she sewed the blue

The Liberty Tree flag was very popular in 1775. New England troops liked their Pine Tree flag. In a battle in South Carolina, an officer carried a red flag cut from the back of a chair. One flag used by the Philadelphia Light Horse Troop was gold in color with 13 alternating blue and white stripes in the upper-left corner. This flag was carried in the battles of Trenton, Princeton, and Germantown.

canton, where the stars would go. Skillfully, she snipped 13 white stars with five points and sewed them in a circle onto the blue background. By the end of June, the flag was done. Betsy delivered it to the committee and hoped that they would be happy with her work. There were many different flags already. She had no idea whether her flag would be the one that people liked the best.

Betsy was just glad to use her talent in a way that helped the American Revolution. The colonies had voted to come together and stand up against Britain. Perhaps a new flag would help them be even more united.

A few days later, Betsy was surprised to hear the bell ringing in the Pennsylvania State House. The sound called the people of Philadelphia into the streets to find out the news. Thousands of people crowded into the yard around the state house. It was July 8, 1776. Only four days earlier, on July 4, the Continental Congress had approved the Declaration of Independence.

Betsy had little time to make the new flag. In order to get the work done quickly, other Patriot women helped her finish the final stitching.

On July 8 it was read publicly for the first time. The Declaration clearly listed the many reasons why the colonies should be totally independent from Britain. It said that all people were entitled to "life, liberty, and the pursuit of happiness." And it was signed by almost all of the members of the Continental Congress.

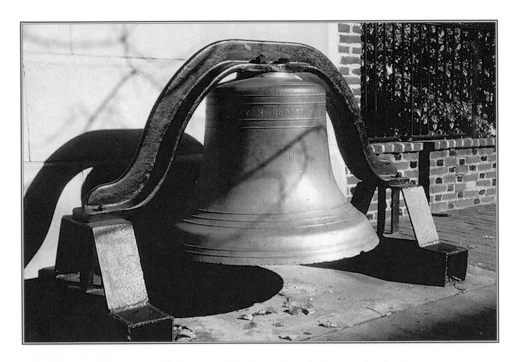

The great bronze Liberty Bell, which Betsy's father had helped to hang in the state house, rang out the news of independence to the citizens of Philadelphia.

After that day, the state house in Philadelphia became known as Independence Hall. And the bell that called the people to hear the news was called the Liberty Bell. Betsy was especially proud because this was the bell that her father had helped to hang many years earlier. Now she had done her part by sewing a flag that would symbolize the new nation.

The Declaration of Independence meant that the 13 colonies officially separated themselves from Great Britain to form a new nation called the United States of America. The American people were prepared to continue to fight the war against Britain. They would fight for as long as they had to in order to protect their independence. Now it was more important than ever for all of the colonies to find a way to work together for their common good.

George Washington, standing in the front of a boat, crosses the frozen Delaware River from Pennsylvania into New Jersey to confront the British. His victory in the battle helped keep Philadelphia safe for a time.

War Comes to Philadelphia

Fighting the Revolutionary War was not easy. By the end of 1776 the British had beaten back the Americans and had taken over much of New Jersey. They were getting ready to attack Philadelphia. Everyone in the city, including Betsy, was preparing for the invasion. George Washington did not want to wait for Philadelphia to be attacked. Instead, he wanted to surprise the British with an attack of his own. But he needed money to do that. He asked his friend Robert Morris to help pay for the battle. Morris borrowed some money from a wealthy Quaker friend and gave it to Washington.

General Washington used this money to pay for the necessary supplies to win a victory against the British. Washington's surprise attack took place on the day after Christmas in 1776. Only four days later the Continental Army went on to win another important victory. The city of Philadelphia was safe—for a while at least. Betsy, along with everyone else there, was very relieved that the immediate threat had passed. Betsy could keep her shop open, even though it became more and more difficult to get the supplies she needed.

On June 14, 1777, something happened that made Betsy very proud. On that day the Second Continental Congress passed a **resolution** that made her flag the one official flag of the newly formed United States of America. The Congressional resolution said, "Resolved That the Flag of the United States be 13 stripes alternate red and white, that the Union be 13 stars white in a blue field representing a new constellation."

Each state was responsible to supply its own

flags for the army. Many flag makers began to make flags. The resolution from the Congress talked about the red and white stripes, but it did not say what the stars should look like. As a result, flag makers put the stars on the flag in any way they liked. Sometimes the stars were in a circle; sometimes they were in rows; sometimes they formed a square. Some of the flag makers made stars that had five points, like Betsy's. Other people made flags with six points or even eight points.

Betsy's sewing business improved quickly after her flag was chosen by the Congress. All of the naval ships needed flags, as did the army troops. Betsy set to work doing her part for the war effort by making lots of flags as quickly as she could.

After the first flag was adopted, it was changed each time a new state joined the Union. In 1795, the flag had 15 stripes and 15 stars. But if a new stripe were added for each new state, either the flag would get too big or the stripes would get too small. So in 1818, Congress decided that the flag should have only 13 stripes in honor of the 13 original states, and a new star would be added for each new state that joined the Union.

As long as flags had the seven red stripes and six white stripes, American flag makers could shape and arrange the stars in any way they wished. The stars in this flag have six points and go across and up and down.

Another big event occurred in Betsy's life the same week that her flag became official. On June 15, 1777, the day after the announcement, she married again. She had been widowed for a year and a half when she found someone to love. His name was Joseph Ashburn. This time

Betsy did not have to sneak off to get married. Her friends and family were with her.

Joseph was muscular and not very tall. He worked on a ship. For a few years, he had his own ship, called the *Swallow*. He sailed the *Swallow* from Philadelphia south to the West Indies in the Caribbean Sea to trade. He brought back shipments of sugar, rum, spices, and molasses.

Joseph was the kind of merchant that the British were unhappy about. He did not follow the rules and bring back only British goods for the colonies. He carried whatever he wanted to on his ship. As the war became more intense, Joseph wanted to do his part to help. He became a privateer. This meant that the Pennsylvania government gave Joseph permission to take over British ships and keep whatever the ships carried. This was very dangerous work, but Joseph and Betsy knew that it was important for American victory.

The years in which Betsy and Joseph were

married were war years. Joseph was away for much of the time. He continued to captain a ship to the West Indies. There he purchased supplies that the people of Philadelphia needed. He also brought back supplies that the army needed. Betsy and Joseph did not have very much time together.

Life in Philadelphia became even more difficult. George Washington had done his best to keep the war away from Philadelphia. But there was hardly any place in the new United States that was not touched by the war.

On August 24, 1777, more than 11,000 American soldiers marched through the streets of Philadelphia. General Washington was preparing to march his troops south to meet the enemy in Maryland. Only 60 miles from Philadelphia, about 17,000 British soldiers waited. They were getting ready to attack. Three weeks later the battle front moved again. This time it was even closer to Philadelphia—only 25 miles away.

The city was in total chaos. Loyalists who supported the British returned to the city, while Patriots who feared for their lives left. Joseph Ashburn was one of the people who decided he must leave to save his ship and his life. Because he was a privateer, he would be put in prison if the British captured him. Betsy knew she had no choice but to let him go. When the British soldiers were in sight she locked herself inside her house. The whole city simply shut down, waiting for the fighting to come to an end.

Life in Philadelphia went from bad to worse. The enemy troops took whatever valuables they wanted. They forced people to take British soldiers into their homes, and they used up the city's precious food supplies. A very cold winter soon arrived. It was impossible to heat the homes. Firewood was difficult to find. British soldiers broke up furniture, doors, and even church pews to burn to keep warm.

Finally, early in June 1778, the British left Philadelphia and headed for New York City.

The British general had learned that the United States was going to get help from Britain's enemy, France. He was afraid that France would invade New York.

It was safe for Joseph to come home again. After a long separation, Joseph returned and was overjoyed to be home with his wife. Betsy was also very happy to see that her husband was safe and well. They had a lot to tell each other about what had happened.

The people of Philadelphia also had a lot of work to do to get their city back to normal. The British left behind a great deal of destruction. Buildings were damaged. Food and other supplies were dangerously low.

Joseph continued sailing his ship between Philadelphia and the West Indies, trading goods, helping in the war effort, avoiding the British, and trying to support his family. Betsy and Joseph's first child, Lucilla, was born on September 15, 1779. They called her Zilla. Soon Betsy was expecting their second child. Joseph left on a trip in October 1780. Both he and Betsy believed that he would be home long before the second baby was born.

But weeks came and went. Joseph did not return. Betsy went down to the docks and talked to other sea captains. She asked if anyone had heard any news of Joseph's ship. No one knew anything about Joseph. But they did know that the British had captured a lot of American ships.

On February 25, 1781, Betsy gave birth to a healthy baby girl, her second daughter, Eliza. Betsy had plenty to do, taking care of two little girls and keeping her busy shop open. But she always wondered what had happened to Joseph. Had he died at sea fighting the British or was he still alive? Did the British have him in a horrible prison somewhere?

Finally the war ended. British General Cornwallis surrendered to the Americans in October 1781. All of the United States celebrated. Betsy was happy the war was over, and she and her

Americans put up a Liberty Pole to celebrate their victory and independence from Great Britain.

two daughters celebrated with their neighbors. She was also sad, though, because Joseph was not there. She wished that they could celebrate together. Joseph had been gone for a year now. She wondered if she would ever see him again.

One day an old friend, John Claypoole, came to visit her. Instead of the happy news that Joseph was on his way home, Betsy learned the sad facts. John Claypoole told Betsy that Joseph's ship had been captured, and Joseph was sent to prison in England. Like Joseph, John was a seaman and a privateer. He had also been captured and put in the same jail as Joseph. This was how John Claypoole had found Joseph. While in prison Joseph had fallen ill and died. He was never able to send word to Betsy or know about the birth of his second child.

Philadelphia was one of the most important
cities in the new United States. Its seaport was
busy with ships coming and going with all kinds
of goods and bringing in many people to live
and work there.

6

A Long, Peaceful Life

John Claypoole continued to call on Betsy Ross. He told her about the British prison and how he and Joseph had met and become good friends there. John and Betsy began to talk about other things too. John had also been brought up as a Quaker. He and Betsy had known each other many years before when they were children. They became good friends as adults. Soon they decided they wanted to be more than friends, and a romance began. On May 8, 1783, Elizabeth Griscom Ross Ashburn married John Claypoole. On that same day John promised to give up the dangers of the sea. He went to work with Betsy in her shop.

Betsy and John Claypoole were married in Christ Church, the same church Betsy had attended with John Ross. Soon Betsy and John decided that they wanted to be Quakers again. Because some Quakers had fought against the British, they did not fit in with the rest of the Society of Friends. They were not allowed to go back to the old Quaker group. So John and Betsy, with Zilla and Eliza, joined the Society of Free Quakers, who had supported the Revolutionary War.

When the peace treaty with Britain was finally signed in 1783, Philadelphia came to life once again. Ships arrived in port with many different things, including a rich variety of fabrics, in all sorts of textures, colors, and patterns. Betsy had everything she needed for her shop. Ships sailed freely between the ports all over the world. For the first time, Philadelphians–including Betsy–would find out what life would

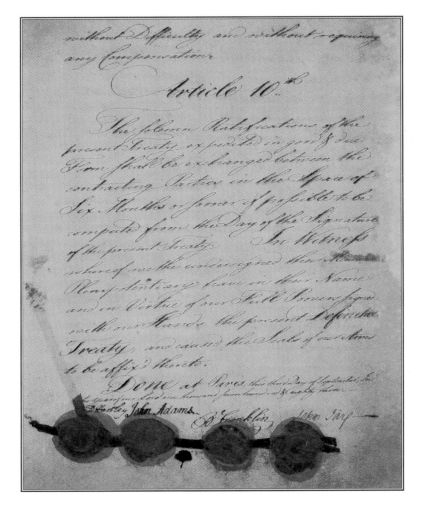

The treaty that brought peace between Britain and the United States was signed in Paris, France.

be like without the British.

Betsy lost two husbands as the new nation struggled to be free. She lived through years of sacrifice and danger. Making the first American flag did not make her famous or wealthy. She was just an ordinary woman who was loyal to her country. She hoped that she could have a long, peaceful life with her husband, John.

There were many brave women who helped to fight and win the Revolutionary War. In 1782, Deborah Sampson, at the age of 22, dressed like a man, changed her name to Robert Shurtleff, and joined the Continental Army. The first time she was wounded, she managed to hide her identity. But then she was wounded again. That time, while being treated in the hospital, a doctor did discover that Deborah was a woman. She was then discharged with honor. After the war she was given a pension.

Soon Betsy and John were adding to their family. Their first daughter was named Clarissa Sidney, after John's sister who had been Betsy's friend during the war years. They called their next daughter Susannah. Before very long, it was clear that the family needed to move to a much larger house. Fortunately they were able to move into the house that Betsy's great-grandfather Andrew Griscom had built.

The family was very

happy to have a bigger house, especially this one. Everyone was giddy with excitement. But there was also one note of sorrow. Zilla, Betsy's oldest child, unexpectedly fell ill and then suddenly died.

Betsy and John had three more daughters, Rachel, Jane, and Harriet. Sadly, Harriet died when she was only a baby. But all the rest of Betsy's children—Eliza, Clarissa Sidney, Susannah, Rachel, and Jane—grew up and had families of their own.

Philadelphia grew up, too. It had been an important city during the war. It was the birthplace of the Declaration of Independence. Then, in November 1790, it became the capital of the United States. Betsy was glad to see George Washington elected as the first president. Her husband was offered a government job at the customs house in Philadelphia, and John happily accepted it. Betsy's shop also did very well. For the next 10 years, the family enjoyed living busy and happy lives in the new nation's capital.

In November 1800, the capital was moved from Philadelphia to Washington, D.C. The president, the Congress, and most government offices left Philadelphia. The city then settled down to a quieter way of life.

Betsy, John, and the entire family faced changes in their home, too. They moved again, to make room for their ever-growing family. The girls grew up and moved out to homes of their own. Then John's health began to fail. The time came when he could no longer work at his job at the customs house. The family once again depended on Betsy's upholstery business. John was sick for many years before he died on August 3, 1817. After losing two husbands while she was young, Betsy had enjoyed being married to John for 34 years.

At the age of 65 Betsy could have closed up her shop and settled in for a quiet retirement. But she did not. Instead, she worked another 10 years. Finally she put away her needles and fabrics, closed her shop, and moved in with her daughter Susannah and Susannah's husband. Later she lived with her daughter Jane and Jane's husband, Caleb Canby.

For as long as she could, Betsy continued to attend meetings of the Society of Free Quakers. But most of the members had drifted away over the years. By 1834 only Betsy and one other member were left. Eventually, they locked the door for the last time. This was the end of the Society of Free Quakers.

In her later years, Betsy enjoyed telling her children and grandchildren stories about her life. She told them about the excitement of defying the British and the hardship of the Revolutionary War. She described what it was like meeting George Washington and the challenge of sewing the very first American flag.

Betsy's children and grandchildren were proud of her and the stories she told them. They were proud that she had accepted the challenge that George Washington, George Ross, and Robert Morris brought her that day in 1776.

Betsy Ross's house in Philadelphia is a historic landmark. Visitors are reminded of her loyalty and her contribution to the cause of American independence.

They were honored that she had played a role in the birth of the new nation.

Betsy became blind in her old age, and it

was very difficult for her to leave the house. Betsy Ross died peacefully on January 30, 1836, at the age of 84.

In 1870 Betsy's grandson William Canby had an idea. He decided that it was time for other people to hear these exciting stories, too. When he was a child at his grandmother's knee, he had heard the story of the first flag. As a grown man, he proudly stood and told the story to a group of people interested in the history of Pennsylvania. Not all people believe William Canby's story. But many people do. And the story of Betsy Ross and the first flag is a good reminder that ordinary people can help change history.

A man named Francis Hopkinson claimed that he made the first flag. Hopkinson served in the Congress and was one of the signers of the Declaration of Independence. After the war Hopkinson asked the Congress for payment for his creation of the first flag. They did not pay him because some thought he was joking.

Hopkinson was a very talented man. He was a poet, musician, composer, inventor, and lawyer. Many people believe that in 1759 he published the first American song. President Washington appointed him a U.S. district court judge in Pennsylvania.

GLOSSARY

ammunition–a supply of bullets and gunpowder to use in guns

Anglican–the major church in Britain

apprentice–a person learning a trade or art from a skilled person

canton–the top corner section of a flag

colony–a land or place ruled by another nation rather than the people who live there

elope–to run away secretly to get married

Free Quakers–Quakers who fought in and actively supported the Revolutionary War

Loyalists–colonists loyal to Britain during the Revolutionary War

militia–a group of civilian men called into the military during emergencies

musket–a gun used by hunters and soldiers before the rifle was developed

pacifists–people who believe in living peacefully and not fighting with others

Patriots–colonists loyal to America during the Revolutionary War; they wanted a new nation

Quaker–a person who belongs to the religious group known as Quakers

resolution–a formal expression of a decision

revolt–an uprising by a group of people against authority

Society of Friends–another name for Quakers, especially those who oppose war

troops–groups of soldiers

upholstery–material used to make soft coverings for furniture

widow–a woman whose husband has died

CHRONOLOGY

1752   Born on January 1 in West Jersey, Pennsylvania.

1754   Family moves to Philadelphia.

1773   Marries John Ross; operates an upholstery shop with husband in Philadelphia.

1776   John Ross dies from injuries in an accident; George Washington asks Betsy to make a flag; American leaders sign the Declaration of Independence.

1777   Betsy's flag becomes the official flag of the United States; marries second husband, Joseph Ashburn; two daughters are born from this marriage.

1782   Joseph Ashburn dies in an English prison.

1783   Marries third husband, John Claypoole; five daughters are born from this marriage.

1817   John Claypoole dies.

1827   Retires and lives with daughters Susannah and Jane.

1836   Dies on January 30.

1870   Grandson William Canby tells her story publicly for the first time.

REVOLUTIONARY WAR TIME LINE

1765   The Stamp Act is passed by the British. Violent protests against it break out in the colonies.

1766   Britain ends the Stamp Act.

1767   Britain passes a law that taxes glass, painter's lead, paper, and tea in the colonies.

1770   Five colonists are killed by British soldiers in the Boston Massacre.

1773   People are angry about the taxes on tea. They throw boxes of tea from ships in Boston harbor into the water. It ruins the tea. The event is called the Boston Tea Party.

1774   The British pass laws to punish Boston for the Boston Tea Party. They close Boston harbor. Leaders in the colonies meet to plan a response to these actions.

1775   The battles of Lexington and Concord begin the American Revolution.

1776   The Declaration of Independence is signed. France and Spain give money to help the Americans fight Britain. Nathan Hale is captured by the British. He is charged with being a spy and is executed.

1777   Leaders choose a flag for America. The American troops win some important battles over the British. General Washington and his troops spend a very cold, hungry winter in Valley Forge.

1778 France sends ships to help the Americans win the war. The British are forced to leave Philadelphia.

1779 French ships head back to France. The French support the Americans in other ways.

1780 Americans discover that Benedict Arnold is a traitor. He escapes to the British. Major battles take place in North and South Carolina.

1781 The British surrender at Yorktown.

1783 A peace treaty is signed in France. British troops leave New York.

1787 The U.S. Constitution is written. Delaware becomes the first state in the Union.

1789 George Washington becomes the first president. John Adams is vice president.

FURTHER READING

Behrens, June. *A New Flag for a New Country*. Chicago: Children's Press, 1975.

Farquhar, Margaret. *Colonial Life in America*. New York: Holt, Rinehart and Winston, 1962.

Fisher, Margaret, and Mary Jane Fowler. *Colonial America*. Fiedeler Co., 1962.

Grote, JoAnn, *The American Revolution*. Uhrichsville, OH: Barbour Publishing, 1997.

St. George, Judith. *Betsy Ross: Patriot of Philadelphia*. New York: Henry Holt and Co., 1997.

Sakurai, Gail. *The Liberty Bell*. New York: Children's Press. 1996.

Steen, Sandra, and Susan Steen. *Independence Hall*. New York: Dillon Press, 1994.

Wallner, Alexandra. *Betsy Ross*. New York: Holiday House, 1994.

Weil, Ann. *Betsy Ross, Designer of Our Flag*. New York: Aladdin Books (Macmillan Publishing), 1983.

INDEX

PICTURE CREDITS

page

ABOUT THE AUTHOR

SUSAN MARTINS MILLER started reading historical stories when she was nine years old. She has written more than 25 books for both children and adults. Her books include fiction, nonfiction, and biography. She lives in Colorado Springs, Colorado, with her husband and two children.

Senior Consulting Editor **ARTHUR M. SCHLESINGER, JR.** is the leading American historian of our time. He won the Pulitzer Prize for his book *The Age of Jackson* (1945), and again for *A Thousand Days* (1965). This chronicle of the Kennedy Administration also won a National Book Award. He has written many other books, including a multi-volume series, *The Age of Roosevelt.* Professor Schlesinger is the Albert Schweitzer Professor of the Humanities at the City University of New York, and has been involved in several other Chelsea House projects, including the Colonial Leaders series of biographies on the most prominent figures of early American history.